# *Freedom from the World*

## Guidance for Christian Living

François Fénelon

REJUVENATED BOOKS

*Series One*

*Freedom from the World*
Rejuvenated Books: Series One
ISBN: 978-1-63171-005-6

*About this text:* François de Salignac de La Mothe-Fénelon was a French archbishop and man of letters whose writings had broad impact on French culture and religion in the seventeenth and eighteenth centuries. His correspondence also provided spiritual guidance to many Christians of the day. The advice presented in this book was originally published in French as *Avis Chrestien*. We have excerpted, arranged, and paraphrased his words from an elderly English translation published in these volumes:

Fénelon, François. *Spiritual Letters of Archbishop Fenelon: Letters to Women*. London: Rivingston, 1877.

Fénelon, François. *Spiritual Letters of Archbishop Fenelon: Letters to Men*. London: Rivingston, 1877.

This book is printed in the United States of America.

# Contents

WHAT YOU ARE experiencing is entirely new to you, an altogether unknown kind of life. You don't recognize yourself. You seem to be dreaming with your eyes open. Accept all of this, but set your heart on nothing. Love, bear your burdens, and continue to love.

# ONE

# Living in the Present

With the past, there is nothing to be done except humbly give it to God, entrusting it to him, and try to make up for past sins with present faithfulness. People want to do things to make up for the past, but what can do that better than simply bearing the responsibilities of the present? The true reparation for former vanity is to become humble and willing to be reduced in your circumstances by God. The most rigorous reparation for past sins is to do what God requires instead of what you want to do — every day and every hour — no matter whether you like it, or grow weary of it, or find it repugnant.

You should pay attention, then, only to the present moment and not let your mind wander curiously into the future. The future is not yours. Perhaps it never will be. You expose yourself to temptation when you try to figure out what God has in store for you and to prepare yourself for something that he may never send you. If he does send you something to do, he will also send you the understanding and strength that it requires. Why should you take on challenges before you are ready, lacking either the understanding or the power to face them? Instead, you should pay close attention to the present moment. Faithful acceptance of present responsibilities is the best way to prepare for the future.

As for the present moment, it seems to me that you only have a few things to think about. The main concerns, as I see it, are as follows.

1. You should avoid not only the company of others who are likely to lead you into actual sins but also of those who might rekindle your appetite for worldly pleasures or who might weaken

you and make you lukewarm toward God, cool in your service to him, indifferent toward the advice you need so much.

2. It's not a good idea, however, in regard to either your outward life or inward life, that you separate yourself entirely from others. Associate with people who don't stir you up during those times when you need to relax. Avoid the people who would distract you and weaken you or who would might reopen old wounds. Separate yourself from false friends like that, avoiding them quietly, putting in place whatever barriers you can between them and yourself.

3. You must strengthen your soul with the word of life. Let your daily reading be both short and long—short when it comes to the number of words but long when it comes to the time you give them. Don't argue with those words. Just love them. You heart—not your head—is required for this kind of reading.

Take what you read and consider your present duties and any faults that you need to correct in order to please God. Don't be afraid to set your book down when God fills your heart with gentleness and devotion. You won't find anything better to read than de Sales. Everything he writes is full of encouragement and love, even though his emphasis is on self-denial. All his works offer profound experiences, humble practices, holy feelings, and the insight that God sends. You take a big step forward when you dine on this kind of intellectual food.

4. As for spending time with God, you won't go wrong by following the good intentions that God has given you — except perhaps by trying too hard. Make it your habit to talk with God not with formal prayers but by putting into words the warm feelings you have for him in your heart. If you feel his presence and are warmed by his love, tell him that. Thank him for accepting a soul that's so unworthy of his love. In those times of almost tangible sweetness, you won't have any trouble pouring out your heart to him.

You might ask, "What should I do when I feel barren, cold, or weary?" You should still say whatever is in your heart. Tell God that you can't feel his love, that you're empty and cold, that he's worn you out, that his presence no longer moves you. Tell him that you would gladly leave him for the weakest worldly pleasures, that you will never be at peace until you are far from him and free to be yourself. Tell him about everything that's wrong within you. Don't be worried about having anything to say. You will have more than enough.

By telling him about your problems, you are asking him to fix them. And to those prayers, add this: "God, just look at my ingratitude, my lack of discipline, my lack of faith! Please take my heart because I can't even give it to you. Watch over it because I can't protect it. Give me whatever worldly problems and burdens are necessary to keep me in line with you. In spite of who I am, please be merciful to me." You can see that you will always have something to say to God.

5

Whether it's about his mercy or your weakness, there will always be plenty to say. In either case, though, talk to him freely about whatever is in your mind with the same sort of intimacy that a child has with its mother.

5. Stay engaged with daily work—managing expenses, watching over your household and your children, maintaining necessary social responsibilities—so that you offer a good example without having to talk about religion. This is all humble and ordinary work, forming for the most part a humble and ordinary life, but it helps to draw you continually closer to God, and you will be greatly comforted and encouraged if you follow this advice because "one day in God's temple is better than a thousand elsewhere."

Two

———————————————————————

# Obedience

Those who have lived far from God imagine that they have drawn very close to him as soon as they make their first steps in that direction. In this way, the most educated and learned people are as mistaken as those peasants who imagine themselves to be members of court because they have seen the king. They renounce their worst, most shocking vices and retreat into a lazy, worldly life of amusement. They judge their new lives not by the gospel, which is the only real standard, but by comparing their new lives to their past lives or to the lives that they see so many others still leading. That is all they need to canonize themselves and then sleep the deepest of sleeps when it comes to everything that is still necessary for them to become holy.

Your holiness does not depend only on ceasing to do what is wrong. You must also learn to do what is right. The kingdom of heaven is too great a prize to be awarded to a simple-minded fear that abstains from wrong-doing merely because it's afraid to commit it. God wants children who love his goodness, not slaves who only serve him because they fear his power. Those who love him naturally do everything that love prompts.

Is it possible to love God with all your heart and still love the world, which is his enemy and which he so severely condemns in his gospel? Can you truly love God and at the same time avoid knowing him more clearly for fear that you might be required to do more to please him? Is it possible to truly love God and at the same time think it's enough to not openly disobey him, while making no effort to please and worship him or tell others of his love? Jesus tells us that the tree that bears no fruit will be cut down and thrown into the fire, and it's true that whoever fails to bear the fruit of divine love is also dead, withered to the root.

Is there any person on earth, however lowly, who is content with being loved no better than with this kind of love that so many offer God? People make a show of loving God with nothing but words and outward tokens. They love God on the condition that they can continue to also love all the worldly vanities that he hates and condemns. Instead of seeing God as the purpose for which they are made, they try to drag him down to their own level. They turn to God only in times of desperation, using him as a thing that helps and comforts them when they fail. Is this really what it means to love God? Isn't it instead a way of attacking him?

A person says, "I have renounced my past sins, I read a little, I go to church, I pray often enough, and I avoid major sins. Beyond that, I don't feel a need to renounce the world or break all contact with it. Your religion must be very strict indeed if it's not satisfied with what I've already done. All your religious rules go too far and tend to discourage people instead of making religion attractive." This is the sort of thing that even well-intended people often say. However, it's easy to enlighten them if they will look honestly at the matter.

The error comes from ignorance of both God and themselves. They are protective of their freedom and fear to lose it by giving too much of themselves to religious life. However, they should remember that they are not their own. They belong to God, and he, having made them solely for himself, has a right to lead them however he wants. They owe their lives to him unconditionally and entirely.

Properly speaking, you don't even own the right to give yourself to God because you don't own yourself. However, if you refuse to leave yourself in God's hands, then you are guilty of the most unholy theft, rebelling from the natural order of things and breaking the basic laws of his creation. It's not your place to argue with the law God gives you. You're required to accept it, treasure it, and follow it blindly. He knows better than you do what's good for you. If you were to write the gospel, you might be inclined to relax its demands a little so as to suit your frailty, but God did not consult you in creating it. He gave it to you fully constructed and gives you no other option to be his than by following this law that applies equally to all people. "Heaven and earth will pass away," but the word of life "will never pass away." Not one word or letter can be set aside. Woe to those religious leaders who take it upon themselves to reduce the weight of this law in order to make it easier for people to follow!

Truly, the God who has this ruling power over his creatures gives them the inner power they need to choose and do what he commands. He makes the burden into something to be loved. He lightens it with inner rewards of justice and truth. He makes virtue delightful with his own presence, and he makes vice disgusting.

He upholds his people as they struggle against themselves, tearing them away from their own corruption, making them strong despite their weakness.

You of little faith, why do you doubt? Leave everything to God. Give yourself to him. You must suffer, but it happens in the midst of love, peace, and encouragement. You must fight, but you win the day, and God, who fights with you, gives you the victory. You must weep, but your tears are not bitter, and God tenderly wipes them away. You're no longer be free to follow your own tyrannical desires, but you freely give up that freedom in order to enter into a new kind of freedom that the world doesn't understand, a freedom in which you're guided entirely by love.

Consider you current bondage to the world. Haven't you already endured much just to win the praise of the people you despise? What has it cost you to repress impulsive desires when they go too far, to yield to others whose approval benefits you, to hide your troubles, or to put up with intolerable social demands? Is this the highly valued freedom that you're so reluctant to sacrifice to God? Where is the freedom? Show it to me. However I look at it, I see nothing but constraint, degrading slavery, a miserable dependence on deception, and dishonesty from morning to night.

Human desires are the harshest of all tyrants. Give in to them just a little, and you'll find yourself in a state of constant conflict, unable to breathe freely even for a moment. They betray and break your heart. They trample down reason and self-respect. They never say "enough." Even if you could count on regular victory over your desires, what sort of victory would that be? And if, on the other hand, you yield to the flood, where will it carry you? I shudder at the thought.

God, save your people from the fatal slavery that human audacity is not ashamed to call "freedom." In you alone can people be free. Your truth will set them free.

The more you love God, the more you love everything that he wants you to do. Love comforts you in your losses, lightens the pain of your sacrifices, loosens your hold on what endangers you, protects you from poisonous traps, and sets before you a tender mercy. No matter what trials come to you—even death itself—love guides you toward the greatness of God and eternal happiness. It transforms every bad thing into good.

God only requires you to perform ordinary tasks—simple, reasonable actions—things that you currently do incorrectly because you don't do them for his sake. He will teach you to do these same things in obedience to him. In this way, even the lowest acts of a simple, ordinary life will be transformed into encouragement, honor, and reward.

# THREE

# Yielding to Love

You must yield to God when he urges you to let him reign within you.

Did you struggle this much when the world tried to seduce you with its enthusiasms and pleasures? Did you hesitate or resist those temptations as firmly as you now resist what is truly good? When it's a matter of straying, getting lost, being corrupted, or acting against your conscience by indulging in sensual pleasures, you're not afraid of going too far. You yield to those temptations without holding back.

However, when it's a matter of believing that you didn't make yourself but are made by an all-wise, all-powerful hand—and then acknowledging that you owe everything to him who made you and gave you everything you have—that's when you start to hesitate, to over-think the situation, to entertain doubts about the simplest, plainest matters. You fear being gullible. You mistrust your experiences. You change your opinions. You worry about giving too much to him for whom nothing can be too much, even though you haven't given him anything yet. You're actually embarrassed to stop being ungrateful and let the world see that you want to serve him. You're as timid about doing what is good as you once were bold in doing what is evil.

All I ask is that you now follow your heart toward what is good in the same way that you once followed your outward desires toward what is evil. When you take a close look at the foundation of your religious training, you see that there's nothing significantly wrong with it. The people who attack it only do so to avoid having to live within its guidelines, rejecting God for the sake of self-satisfaction. Is it right to be so open when it comes to the self and so narrow when it comes to God? Do you really need to reason so much just to understand that God made you not for yourself but for him?

What do you risk by serving him? You want to continue to do whatever is appropriate and lawful—just like before. You want to bear the same responsibilities and suffer the same problems. The difference is that you will now have the great pleasure of loving the one who is so worthy of your love, of working and suffering in order to please a true friend. This friend cares about everything in your life, however small, and rewards your sacrifices a hundred times over—in *this* life—with a peace that fills your heart. Above all that, you gain the promise of an eternal and wonderful life with him. Compared to that, all that you have here is nothing more than a slow death.

Don't argue with God. Either listen to your own heart, in which God is now speaking to

you lovingly in spite of your past unfaithfulness, or talk with any of your friends who
are sincerely committed to God. Ask them
what they think about serving God. Ask them
whether they regret having made this decision
or whether they were too gullible or headstrong
in making it. They, like you, were people of the
world. Ask them if they regret leaving the world
behind and whether the pleasure of Babylon is
sweeter than the peace of Zion.

Whatever suffering may come from living a
Christian life, you won't ever have to lose that
wonderful peace of heart. It allows you to accept
any suffering that God sends and reject any
happiness that he holds back. Can the world give
you anything like that? Are worldly people ever
satisfied with what they have? Are they moti-
vated by this kind of love in their hearts? You
know the answer.

What are you so afraid of? Are you afraid of
leaving something that will soon leave you — that
is, in fact, already slipping away? A worldly life

can never fill your heart. Instead, it turns into a deadly weariness and creates within you an emptiness, a secret self-loathing. Even while it dazzles you, it remains worthless.

What are you so afraid of? Are you afraid of following too much goodness, of finding a too-loving God, of being pulled forward by something that is stronger than yourself or the charms of this poor world?

What are you so afraid of? Are you afraid of becoming too humble, too pure, too true, too reasonable, too grateful to your father in Heaven?

Don't be afraid of anything so much as this false fear — this foolish, worldly wisdom that can't decide between God and the self, between right living and sinful living, between gratitude and ingratitude, between life and death. You know from your own experience what it means to waste away because you lack an inner life that is fed by love. You become lifeless and lose heart without that indescribable *something* that sustains you, upholds you, and renews you hour by hour.

In a way, everything that the crazed lovers of the world say about love is true. To be without love is to be without life. To love weakly is to waste away instead of grow. All the wild passions that pull people here and there are simply cases where true love has strayed from its proper goal. God created you to live with him and with his love. You are born to be both fed and consumed by that love in the same way that a torch is consumed as it gives off light. This is the wonderful fire of life that God has kindled in the bottom of your heart. Any other kind of life is merely death. You must love!

What then will you love? Will you love something that doesn't love you, that isn't lovable, that has no more substance than a shadow?

What will you love in this world? Will you love people who are jealous of you, who fume with envy when they discover that you're content? Will you love hearts that are as hypocritical in worldly matters as the devout are accused of being in religious matters?

What will you love? Will it be a worldly dignity that might easily slip away and can't offer any real comfort when you have it? Will you love the approval of a blind world, even though you despise the individuals within it? Will you love this body of clay that restrains your intellect and subjects you first to disease and then to death?

Will you love nothing? Will you struggle through a lifeless existence instead of loving the God who loves you, who seeks your love, who wants you to be entirely his so that he can give himself entirely to you? How can you worry about lacking anything in this life when you have such a treasure as that? Don't you believe that the infinite God can fill and satisfy your heart?

Never count on yourself or on anything else in this world, which all adds up to nothing. It can never satisfy the heart because the heart is made for God. Instead, you should always count on God, in whom all good things are found. He fills you with disgust for anything else in order to forcibly bring you back to himself.

# Four

# Giving Yourself to God

God's way of life is pleasing and satisfying to those who look for it with love in their hearts. The more you give yourself to God, the more he gives himself to you, and every step you take toward him brings peace and encouragement to your heart. However, this dedication to God—which many people are afraid of, worrying that it will be an annoying burden—is only true dedication when it encourages you to continue moving forward.

To the degree that your work for God increases, your weariness disappears. You never get tired of doing what you like to do. When you have to do something difficult for the sake of the one you love, your love softens the hardship and makes you want to bear it. You wouldn't be relieved by setting that burden down. Instead, your satisfaction comes from sacrificing yourself for the sake of your beloved. The more you give yourself entirely to Jesus, the more you are satisfied by following the one you love. And what more could you ask than to always be content with your work, to never bear any cross except for the one cross that is more satisfying than worldly pleasures? You will never find that kind of satisfaction from yielding to your own desires, nor will you fail to find it as long as you sincerely seek God.

It's true that this kind of satisfaction isn't always physical and obvious — the kind of satisfaction you experience with worldly pleasures — but it's still very real and superior to anything that the world has to offer. Worldly people always crave the thing they don't have and thus are never satisfied. You, however, moved by your love for God, only desire what you already have. Your peace might sometimes seem a little dull, and even tinged with difficulty at times, but it remains more satisfying to the soul than any physical pleasures. It's a peace that puts you at one with yourself, a peace that is never broken or troubled except by unfaithfulness. The more you're faithful to the one you love, the more you enjoy this blessing of peace. The world can't give you this kind of peace, nor can it take it away. If you don't believe that, test it for yourself. Taste and see how good the Lord is.

One of the best things you can do now is to set aside some time each day to spend with God. Read a little, and then meditate quietly — asking forgiveness for your shortcomings, considering your work, looking to God, and developing the habit of intimate conversation with him. It isn't helpful to merely ask people who love God what they do with him. How happy will you be to discover for yourself what it means to make this love your occupation.

You don't have any problem spending time with a friend you love. Your heart is always ready and open. You don't have to figure out what you will say. It just comes to you without planning. You can't hold back. Even if you have nothing in particular to say, you still like to be with that friend.

How much easier it is to love than to fear! Fear holds you back, imprisons you, and perplexes you, but love encourages, comforts, enlivens, and expands your soul. It makes you desire what is good for its own sake. It's true that you always need the fear of God's judgment as a counterbalance against worldly desires — "My flesh trembles for fear of You" and "May my whole body be filled with your fear, O Lord" — but though you begin this journey with fear that subdues the body, you must move on to the love that encourages the soul. What a good and faithful friend you will find in God if you form a sincere, on-going friendship with him.

If you decide to give yourself entirely to God, the first thing to do is to stop relying on your own abilities, given the many experiences you've had with your *in*abilities, and then to remove yourself from the company of anyone who might pull you back into your former ways. If you want to love God, why would you want to spend your life with those who don't love him—or who even despise his love? Wouldn't it be better to instead spend your time with those who also love him, and who will help you grow in your love for him?

I'm not asking you to entirely reject your old friends, nor to avoid the people brought into your life by circumstances. This is more a matter of avoiding close friendships with people who tend to soil the character of others, who almost unconsciously drag you down in spite of your good intentions. This also means cutting back on the time you spend with vain people who are devoted entirely to impressing others, who hunger for worldly pleasure, who make fun of a life of faith, and who encourage dangerous distractions. That kind of company is hazardous even for people who are firmly established in a good life and much more so for people like yourself who are taking their first steps in the right direction and are still naturally inclined toward traveling in the wrong direction.

Beyond that, you should also take seriously the problem of lingering in your own bad habits and thus abusing the generous opportunity that God has given you. God has waited for you, sought you out, invited you, urged you — one could even say *forced* you — to return to him. Isn't it right, then, for you to come to him now? Shouldn't you now turn away from your old habits and desires, especially considering how dangerous they can be? Shouldn't you turn away from former sins? And shouldn't that rejection of old ways bring into your life humility and self-control when it comes to worldly company? The wise man says, "He who loves danger will die in that danger." No matter what it costs, you must reject those old sins and the opportunities to commit them. We are bound by the words of Jesus to cut off a hand or pluck out an eye if it traps us or makes us stumble back into sin.

That being said, you don't have to publicly announce the exchange of your former life for a new life in Jesus and thus open yourself up to mean-spirited gossip. True religion never requires publicity. Two things are enough. First, never set a bad example for others that makes you feel guilty in the presence of Jesus and in the new life he offers you. Second, do whatever God's love requires of you but do it simply and without showing off.

To follow the first rule, you should attend church services with the proper respect, and no matter where you find yourself, you must never speak well of bad behavior nor participate in idle or indecent conversation. To follow the second rule, your study, prayers, confessions, communions, and other good works should all be private. By following these rules, you avoid spiteful attacks from worldly people without yielding to a false sense of shame or timidity that will quickly drag you back down into the rushing stream of a world life, a stream that will sweep you away.

The most important step for you to take is to quietly step away from any distractions that you have particular reason to fear. Limit yourself socially, too, keeping company with a few chosen friends who think in the way that you desire to think for the rest of your life.

# FIVE

# Holding Back

By now, you can have no doubts about how worthless the world is, how it can never make you happy, how its flattering promises are nothing more than lies and delusions. You also understand what rights the creator has over his creatures and how inexcusable ingratitude toward the creator is — much worse than ingratitude toward people in the world. Furthermore, you have experienced God for yourself through all that he has done and through the generous peace with which he fills those who love him. With all of this in mind, what could possibly hold you back except for your love of independence and your unwillingness to learn?

You shy away from having to obey to him. That's the true nature of these doubts that you pretend are holding you back. You try to convince yourself that you don't believe firmly enough, and that because of these doubts, you couldn't take any step toward God without blindness and the risk of backsliding.

However, no actual doubts about the truth of Christianity cause your indecision. It is instead your indecision that grasps at this pretext of doubt as a way to delay the obedience that your natural self finds so disagreeable. People exaggerate their doubts in order to release themselves from having to do anything, from having to give up the worthless independence that their natural selves cling to so jealously. Be honest. What real problems do you have to offer? There aren't any except for your fear of restraint and having to lead what you worry will be a dull, boring life, that you will be led farther down the path toward holiness than you want.

You hold yourself back because you're learning to appreciate the true nature of a religious life, to feel its claims on you, and to see the sacrifices that it inspires in others. However, what you haven't yet learned is the attractive, happy side of religious life. You see what it requires, but you don't yet see what it offers. You thus exaggerate its sacrifices without understanding its rewards.

This life leaves no emptiness in your heart. It offers you rewards that you will learn to prefer to anything you've known. If the world never required anything of you except for what your heart could lovingly accept, wouldn't it be a better master than it actually is? In contrast, God watches over you, waits for you, prepares you, and gives you the desire to obey before he asks you to do anything. Just as he restrains your worldly inclinations, out of love, he gives you a desire for truth and goodness that is stronger all your former desires.

What are you waiting for? Do you wait for him to send miracles to convince you? No miracle will conquer indecision that arises from the self-love that you're afraid to sacrifice. Do you wait for endless arguments while, in your heart, you already understand what God wants from you? Arguments will never heal the wound in your heart. You argue not to reach a conclusion so that you can do something but to create for yourself the excuse of doubt so that you can delay doing anything. What you deserve is for God to leave you to yourself as punishment for this prolonged resistance of yours. Even so, in his mercy, God pursues you and troubles your heart so that you might surrender it to him and put an end to your dangerous indecision.

What seems to you like wavering between two paths is in fact taking the wrong path. Your outward deliberation is the inward decision to be ruled by self-love, to avoid any sort of discipline. You have argued too much already. If you really have any actual, intellectual problems, then put them down in writing and we will go over them carefully together. If, on the other hand, you have only a vague sense of doubt that arises from your reluctance to be ruled by faith, then why delay submitting?

Quiet your intellect. Is it any wonder that the infinite God is more than your weak, narrow mind can understand? Would you limit God and his mysteries to what you can understand? Would he be infinite if you could comprehend everything about him? Do justice to yourself, and you will soon do justice to him. Humble yourself, mistrust yourself, look at yourself as the weak human that you are. Acknowledge the dullness of your mind and the weakness of your heart. Instead of sitting in judgment over God, let him judge you.

Tell God that you need him—desperately—to watch over you and guide you. There's no greatness so real as this inward humility that knows its own limitations. There's no argument so reasonable as the honest acknowledgment of a lack of wisdom. Nothing is worthy of God except for the quiet awareness on your

part of intellectual weakness and your willing-
ness to set aside false understandings. Nothing is
so enlightened as a humble soul. Once it sees its
own darkness, it will soon see the truth.

# Six

# Drawing Closer to God

It doesn't surprise me that you find yourself disgusted with so many things that displease God. It's a natural result of the change God brings to your heart. You prefer a quiet situation that allows you to focus on what you enjoy the most and escape anything that might reopen old wounds, but that's not what God gives you. He instead chooses to keep you where you are so that the things that once engaged you so much might now become wearisome and help to purify you. Bear that cross patiently to make amends for past sins and wait for God to remove it. He will—but according to his own timing, not yours.

In the meantime, take time for yourself and use it to draw closer to God. Read, pray, and distrust your natural inclinations and habits. Remember that you are like a clay pot into which God has poured his most precious gift, so above all, strengthen that inner life by staying in his love. Even though your former ways were far from God, don't worry about approaching him with intimate love.

In your prayer, talk to him about your weaknesses, your deficiencies, your troubles—even the weariness you feel in serving him. It's impossible speak to him with too much openness or too much trust. He loves the gentle and humble and is always ready to talk with them. Open your heart and tell him everything. Then wait and listen to him. Let your whole being listen in silence for his voice. This kind of silence—shutting out the outward life, ordinary feelings, and human thoughts—is essential if you want to hear the voice that calls the soul to die to itself and live for God in spirit and truth.

You have read a great deal, so you understand the principles of religion and the arguments that can be made against it. However, all this learning, which at first leads you to God, will after a while hold you back if you trust your own understanding too much. You must be like a small child. The humility in children far exceeds the greatness of the great—happy are those who find it! To argue, reason, discuss, and decide isn't worth much. The main thing is to love the only one who is true and good and to plant yourself firmly in that love.

This isn't a matter of doing something difficult and unusual for God. Do the smallest, most ordinary things with a heart that seeks God as its only goal. You can then do anything that others do—other than sin, of course. You will then be a kind, cheerful, polite, and willing friend, one who is happy at such times and in such company as is appropriate for a Christian. You will be in control of yourself in social situations and everywhere else—in your speech, your expenses, your decisions, your working with others, your entertainments, and even in religious matters. The love of God teaches this self-control in all things, even the best things, with beautiful simplicity. Those who learn this self-control are never rigid, harsh, or anxious. They're guided instead by a love that expands the heart, softens it, and fills it—generously and without anxiety—with a sensitive desire to never offend God.

People who are guided by love in this way still suffer at times—like the rest of the world—from weariness, struggles, self-doubt, bad attitudes, physical ailments, inward frustrations, outward frustrations, temptations, discouragement, and weakness. However, although these crosses are common to everyone, the motivation to endure is different when you're guided by love. You understand the value and goodness of bearing the cross of Jesus, how it purifies, removes worldliness, and renews. You can see God at work in any circumstance, but you never see him so clearly or beneficially as you do in suffering and weakness. The cross is God's great power at work in this world. The more it bruises, the more your new self in Jesus emerges from the ruins of old Adam. Continue then without making any outward changes except for whatever is necessary to avoid falling back into sin.

If you can find a reasonable, God-fearing friend, you can lighten your mind by talking over matters that your friend can appreciate, but always remember that God remains your best friend and that no one can comfort you as well as he can. No one else can understand without the need for words. No one else can visit you in all your worries and take care of all your needs without growing tired of them. Let God be like a second self to you, and soon that second self will replace the first self and set it aside entirely.

Watch over your daily work and your expenses. Be honorable, modest, humble, and impartial. Serve others out of duty rather than from ambition or fierce hopes of advancement. That is how you should serve your country, your king, and the king of kings. Compared to him, all worldly majesty is just a shadow. This kind of impartial service will help to make up for the showing off and shameless ambition of past service.

Maintain a consistent, simple course of action, without an outward show of good or bad but with a firm commitment to what is right—firm enough that there will be no chance of dragging you back into old ways. You will escape that threat and be less worried when others see that you really are devoted to religion and that you will not yield. People suspected of weakness, inconsistency, or insincerity are sure to be surrounded by constant demands. Don't depend on your own strength or resolve, nor on any promises you make, nor on the best possible precautions—although you should also take careful precautions. Depend entirely on God's goodness. Remember that he loved you before you loved him. He loved you even when you were ungrateful to him.

# SEVEN

# Understanding
# Your Responsibilities

You would like to believe that you can be content with doing what you already understand without trying to understand your responsibilities more clearly, but I disagree.

I don't propose the kind of excessive, unwise slavery to rules that forces you to worry about everything, no matter what you do, for fear that it might be wrong. God forbid that I should burden you with a timid, fearful religion that believes that God pardons nothing, that he is always waiting to pounce on your most trivial faults in order to reject you entirely! I don't know of anything so harmful as that kind of religion. Instead of forcing that on you, I would like to you to be guided by pure love, which is always comfortable, relaxed, cheerful, brave, and enlivened with confidence.

However, you must still consider honestly the responsibilities you owe to God. Don't you owe as much to God as a friend owes to friends or a servant owes to a master? If you have friends whom you trust entirely and love tenderly, friends who owe you the deepest obligations, will you be satisfied if they only listen to a fraction of what you ask of them? What will you think of them or their friendship if they follow the general idea of what you request but avoid learning the details?

Will any of your friends really deserve to be called friend and will you believe in the friendship if one says, "I'm doing what I imagine you require of me. What more do I need to know? More information might be inconvenient, so I'm not going to bother with that. I would rather harm your interests a little than take on the burden of a more detailed understanding."

Surely such "friends" would be unworthy of that name. You would be deeply wounded by their ingratitude and feel ashamed for having trusted them. In fact, you'd find this conduct worse because they added bad faith to bad intentions. You'd prefer them to openly refuse to serve you than to offer their services and then ignore your interests and hide from you so that they didn't have to do too much. That's inexcusable.

For another example, suppose that a king has entrusted a fortress, or an army, or a diplomatic negotiation to one of his subjects. Will he be satisfied if that commander neglects to inform him about the condition and strength of the fort? Will he be satisfied if his general is content to know only a small part of the war plan? Will he be satisfied if his diplomat refuses to learn about the details of the foreign matter or how to conclude a succession agreement?

If the king later confronts these servants with their failure, the commander won't dare to say, "I thought I knew enough, even though I didn't understand sieges or bother to learn more so that I could hold the fort." Nor can the ignorant general answer, "I didn't wish to bother myself with the various opinions of those planning the defense, nor to discuss the matter with other officers who could have enlightened me because of their own experiences. I meant well. I thought my good intentions and limited understanding would be sufficient." As for the diplomat, can he claim that he wasn't bound to understand an enemy's plan, nor to study the politics of the nation to which he was sent, nor to consider the methods by which he might secure his king's goals? Surely the king will tell all three of his servants, "You should have studied day and night to figure out these matters. Your neglect was a betrayal of my interests. You sacrificed my interests to your laziness." What then, will the King of Kings say to you if you are like these bad servants?

The observation of the Lord's day was specifically established so that there would be one day each week set aside for studying God's law and meditating on his truths. And in the past, those who became Christians were given a long course of instruction before they were allowed to be baptized. The need to know God and Jesus Christ, our savior, is every bit as important now and can never be less important. The gospel with which God teaches us is not given to us as a closed book.

I know that there are evil-minded, untrained people who might misuse their knowledge of the gospel, but those who are being trained with good intentions and an open mind should not deprive themselves of its use. You can be sure that we will be judged by that book, not by people. Therefore, we should prepare to account for ourselves according to the rules of that book, which are God's rules.

Paul tells the early Christians, "In Jesus, you are made rich in all ways, in every word of doctrine and in all knowledge." Nevertheless, he continually teaches them that they need to grow daily in their knowledge of God, to be filled with his light so that they will know what he desires clearly and completely and thus become fruitful in all that they do. Jesus teaches the responsibility for careful study of his law, and judges even the sources of instruction, when he says, "If the blind lead the blind, they will both fall into a ditch." Notice that he doesn't say that one will excuse the other.

Avoid teachers who are rigid in their outward forms of religion, harsh practices, or love of novelty, but also beware of flattering counselors, worldly ones who "sew magic bracelets for every wrist" instead of teaching repentance. Use all the wisdom God gives you to find a happy medium. Look for a spiritual guide as carefully as worldly people seek the best lawyer or doctor. Then you can rest satisfied and trust the goodness of God, who will not allow you to be lost, even if you are mistaken in your choice.

Must you spend your entire life in religious study like a professor? No. That isn't what God requires of you. He requires you to feed your soul each day with the truths of his gospel, not to make you arrogant but to give you a more informed mistrust of self so that you can learn from Jesus to be "meek and humble of heart." You won't learn from the gospel the sort of knowledge that puffs up your vanity. The gospel instead teaches you to despise self, to trample the worthless treasures of the world, to leave behind a fleeting and uncertain kind of life, to seek God's enduring goodness, and to be gentle, patient, just, and honest with others.

Such knowledge is not acquired by careful reasoning, serious reading, or a powerful memory. All you need is a simple, teachable spirit that will go deeply into the study of godliness without any unusual cleverness. You will learn the most profound truths from a few words. If you are truly humble, you will know more than the most learned of proud scholars. This is why

*Freedom from the World*

Jesus says, "I thank you, Father, because you have hidden these things from the wise and learned and have revealed them to children," and, "Unless you become childlike, you will not enter the kingdom of heaven." The understanding you should seek in your daily consideration of God's word is how to be as humble as a little child.

# Judging Others

You are overwhelmed by your failings and your powerlessness to conquer them. Such despair, when your natural person is so reduced that you expect nothing from yourself and hope only in God, is exactly what God wants. He will improve you when you give up the hope of improving yourself. God does not judge you for your natural character, which you do not choose for yourself and cannot choose to set aside. Indeed, these tendencies help to bring you into holiness if you bear them as a cross.

What God *does* require is that you do whatever his grace puts in front of you. You have to be humble inwardly if you cannot be gentle outwardly. You have to drop your natural, proud behavior as soon as you become aware of it and with gentleness make up for any harm your pride may have done. You have to steadily and patiently practice humility when the opportunity arises. You have to set aside your own strong opinions with all sincerity.

It is time now for you to be humbled by your own failings, just as, in the past, your attention to the failings of others made you proud. Make it a habit to notice when people care little for your ideas, and work hard to not criticize them. The same self-love that causes your failings subtly moves you to hide them from others and from yourself. Self-love can't bear to see itself. The sight overwhelms it with shame and frustration. If self-love accidentally catches a glimpse of itself, it looks for some false light that will soften and condone what it finds so hideous. As long as you retain any love for yourself, you also maintain illusions about yourself.

To see yourself perfectly, your self-love must be rooted out, and the love of God must have full dominion over you. Then the same light that exposes your failings also removes them. Until then, you only half know yourself because you only half give yourself to God, clinging to self much more than you think or dare to admit. When you "receive all truth," you see clearly. When you love yourself only with the love of mercy, you see yourself as you see your neighbor — without self-interest and without flattery.

In the meantime, God spares you from your weakness, only showing you your true wretchedness in proportion to the courage he gives you to bear the sight. He shows you one small part, and then another, as he gradually leads you to change. Without this merciful preparation, with light given in proportion to strength, the sight of your frailty would only lead to despair.

You need more generosity when it comes to the failings of others. True, you can't help but to see the failings when they are forced upon you. You can't *not* arrive at obvious conclusions about the faulty principles that guide some. You can't avoid the annoyance that these things cause. However, you do need to be content to bear with the obvious failings of others, to avoid judging those with faulty principles, and to resist the annoyance that estranges you from people.

Holiness finds it easy to bear with the failings of others, to be "all things to all people." You should learn how to put up with the most obvious faults in worthy people, leaving them alone until God shows you that it's time to gradually weed out those failings. Otherwise, you are likely to pull out the grain with the weeds. Another reason to be patient with others is that God often leaves certain weaknesses in the lives of even the most advanced souls, weaknesses that seem quite out of character in those lives. In clearing fields for planting, some workers leave tokens of what they've cleared to show how extensive their work has been. In the lives of these more advanced, God often leaves tokens like this to show how far he has brought them.

All people must labor at self-improvement to the best of their ability, and you must labor to be patient with the imperfections of others. Your own experience teaches you that correction can be a bitter thing. Because you know this, work hard to soften any of your correction for others. What moves you to act may not be so much a passion to help others improve as an aversion to their failings, an aversion that shuts your heart to them.

If you do find any failing in someone, present it openly for what it is. You may offer a suggestion but don't otherwise warn or condemn. Be as ready and willing to be judged yourself as you are to judge others. Your goal is to put yourself on the same level with the most humble and weak. Allow them to be free and open with you, and if you have anything to offer them, do so not so much to correct them but to encourage and strengthen them.

All other methods of guidance to others feel like earthly judgments instead of gracious corrections because they are given impatiently and out of frustration with the failings. Imperfection is correcting the imperfect. It is a crafty, clinging self-love that sees nothing to forgive in the self-love of others. The greater your own self-love, the more severe you are as a critic.

The love of God, on the other hand, is full of thoughtfulness, patience, humility, and tenderness. It adapts itself to the person. It waits, never moving more than one step at a time. The less self-love you have, the more you understand how to adapt yourself to the work of healing your neighbor's failings. You understand better that you never lance a wound without first applying plenty of healing ointment, you never purge patients without first feeding them, and you never risk an operation except when the situation suggests the operation is best. You learn to wait for years before giving a healthy warning, to wait until providence prepares the right outward circumstances and grace opens the hear. If you keep gathering fruit before it's ripe, you're simply wasting your labors.

As for your imperfect friends, they can only know you imperfectly. They judge you simply because of outward failings that affect them socially or that jar their own self-love. Self-love is a sharp, harsh, and unforgiving critic, and the same self-love that softens their view of their own failings makes them magnify yours. Because their point of view is entirely different from yours, they see things that you don't see in yourself and overlook many things that you do see.

They are quick to notice many things that wound their sensitive, jealous self-love — and that your own self-love conceals — but they don't see the hidden failings that further darken your virtue and that only God sees. Therefore, even their wisest judgment is superficial. My opinion is that it's best to instead listen to God in a deep, inward silence. In all humility, accept whatever judgment—for you or against you—that his light reveals when you open your heart to him.

NINE

# Anxiety

Nothing is so damaging to unity with God as an anxious mind. It provides cover for all sorts of falsehood and duplicity. You imagine that all your anxiety comes from your sensitive love of God, but in reality, there is a great deal of self-focus in it, the fond pursuit your own self-improvement and human self-interest. You thus deceive yourself to your own harm and turn away from God under the pretext of being cautious.

Love is friendly and intimate. It doesn't hold back. It doesn't deceive. It sits out in the open in all your interactions with the beloved. If you find yourself growing anxious about your relationship with God, you should suspect that something other than love is dividing the heart, restraining it, and causing it to hesitate. You don't focus so much and so anxiously on your own spiritual state unless you are clinging to some other passion and thus putting limits on your union with the beloved.

Worries about doing what's right will damage you permanently if you continue to listen to them. That turns into true faithlessness. You are wise to let go of them. If you don't, you offend the Holy Spirit. "Where the Spirit of the Lord is, there is freedom," but where constraint, anxiety, and fearfulness are, there is willfulness and conceited concern for yourself. How different is true love from these problems. Those who are so wrapped up in their own fancies care little about the beloved.

Trust love. It requires everything from you, but it also gives everything to you. It leaves nothing in the heart except itself. It allows nothing other than itself, but it satisfies every longing because it comprises everything. Those who taste it are drunk with a sweetness that is still only a foretaste of the heavenly joy that waits for you. This experience of love seizes and absorbs and makes the soul care nothing about the loss of everything.

These words often apply to you: "As water puts out fire, so anxiety puts out the spirit of prayer." Don't indulge in anxiety so much, and you *will* find rest. These problems with which you reproach yourself are nothing more than trivialities, without any malice in them, and entirely harmless to others. There is nothing in this that should trouble you so much. These trifles arouse your anxiety, and your anxiety disturbs your prayer. It pulls you away from God, withers and distracts your soul, opens the door to worldly inclinations, and awakens temptation in spite of God's grace. See how much worse the remedy is than the disease? The disease is imaginary, but the remedy is a real and evil.

*Freedom from the World*

There are two things that should help you to clear away all your fears. The first thing is your awareness of your own excitability and your great skill in tormenting yourself about nothing. The second thing is recognizing the harm that these anxieties do to you. Every time that you launch into these self-investigations, you distract and trouble yourself. You move farther from the power of prayer, and thus from God. You become entirely self-absorbed. I ask you, is any of this from God? Do you see his hand in it? Does love make you stop loving?

Isn't it wrong in God's eyes for you to give up close communion with him in order to indulge yourself with an anxious search for any trifling fault within yourself, which you then enlarge in your imagination? Suppose that you take these trifles at their worst and grant that they are actual sins. Even then, they are easily forgivable sins. You should humble yourself and work to correct them, but you can easily erase them with a loving prayer.

Can it be right, under the pretext of hunting for the smallest faults, that you dry up the springs of prayer within you? Can it be right to do yourself so much harm in order to cure so little? Anxieties over trifles are illusions of evil in the same way that false prayers are illusions of good. There is no illusion in believing without seeing, in loving without selfishness, in receiving without holding back from what is given, in renouncing everything that comes from the self.

Your problems actually come from a lack of faith. If you had not pulled back from God in order to follow your own plans, you would not have suffered in this way. There is no greater evil than these attempts of yours to attain an imaginary relief. Patients with dropsy only increase their thirst by drinking, and in the same way, victims of these anxieties only increase their problems by worrying about them.

The more you yield to anxiety, the more you develop it. You can only cure it by repressing it. When you finally conquer it, you will find peace. This peace is not just calmness, either, but an enlightened spiritual state that allows you to more clearly understand how to avoid the trap of anxiety. This peace bears good fruit. It confirms that God is guiding you.

TEN

# Self-indulgence

Self-indulgence and the love of amusement are enough to derail you even when you're the most determined to do what's right and avoid what's wrong. Self-indulgence numbs your soul and removes all energy for doing good. It's a treacherous weakness that secretly spurs the soul to sin, hiding a consuming fire beneath its seemingly mild ashes. You need a vigorous, strong faith to constantly protect against this easy softness. If you try to negotiate with it even once, all is lost.

Self-indulgence is as mischievous in worldly matters as it is in spiritual matters. Self-indulgent people are barely people at all. They become poor, weak creatures. The love of ease overpowers their own best interests. They don't develop their talents or acquire the knowledge they need for a profession. They don't take on the regular work of a challenging position, or work with the tastes and dispositions of others, or try to correct their own failings. They're like the sluggard of scripture who "desires much and has nothing." They want to do what's right when it's far off, but when they come face to face with the work, they fall back lazily.

What can you do with people like this? They're fit for nothing. They would happily spend their whole lives in beds of down! When they work, the minutes seem like hours. When they amuse themselves, the hours pass like minutes. Time glides past them like water under a bridge. Ask them: "How did you spend the day?" They can't tell you because they've spent their time without actually living. They slept as late as they could, dressed slowly, gossiped with anyone who turned up, dawdled about their room, perhaps lazily attended mass. Then came dinner. The evening went like the morning. Their whole lives are like that day.

I'll say it again — the self-indulgent are good for nothing. They are not merely incapable of doing any good but are sure to gradually fall into great sin. Pleasure betrays them. The self cannot be indulged without penalty. For a time, self-indulgence might seem painless and passive, but in a moment, it becomes become brutal and violent. The flame beneath the ashes doesn't show itself until it's too late to put it out.

You must watch yourself. Even your religious training, when mixed with self-indulgence, gradually leads you into a way of life that outwardly appears to be disciplined but inwardly is hollow. You might take great pride in giving up the company you kept in your early, foolish days but not see that you are merely using religion to disguise the fact that you are giving them up because they bore you, or because you're less popular, or because you're not flashy enough for them. Religion may lead you toward a more sober and quiet life, but don't let that life be just as hollow and unreal as the other.

Grossly self-indulgent people, whose desires triumph over them, lead vile and wretched lives that even the world in its worldliness despises. With this kind of self-indulgence, you may gradually leave the world — not for God, though, but for your own desires or for a life of ease that is opposed to God and that the world itself looks down on as worse than the greatest corruption.

How can you guard against self-indulgence? First, make a plan for using your time wisely and stick to that plan at all costs. Next, the most important part of this plan should be to spend a half hour every day in meditative reading. During that time, always remember to renew your resolution to not be self-indulgent. Third, examine yourself every evening to see whether you have yielded to self-indulgence and lost track of your time. Fourth, go regularly every other week to some confessor who understands your tendency toward self-indulgence and who will help you to keep up a vigorous struggle against it. Fifth, if possible, ask a good friend to warn you privately when you appear to be giving way to self-indulgence. To benefit from these warnings, though, you must seek them in earnest and let people see that you are glad to receive their warnings and are trying to respect them. Never be petty or arrogant when you receive these warnings.

In the morning, make time for your reading and meditation from the hours when you are supposed to be in bed. Read again in the evening, and if you feel up to it, gather yourself inwardly while doing so. You will gradually get into the habit of making a short meditation then as well as in the morning. However, don't work too hard at this at first so that you don't grow weary of prayer. During mass, you might read the epistle and gospel in order to unite yourself to the priest in thinking about the great sacrifice of Jesus. Turning your thoughts there helps you to keep your mind lifted up to God.

Finally, remember that self-indulgence numbs and weakens everything, stripping away all power and life from your mind and body—even from the world's point of view. Those who yield to self-indulgence are small and weak in everything, so lukewarm that God rejects them. The world does the same, too, because it has nothing say to anyone but the active and lively. Self-indulgent people are thus shunned both by God and by the world. They become nothings, ignored and despised.

Beware of this failing, this source of so much evil. Pray. Guard yourself against self. Pinch yourself like you might pinch some who is sleeping. Get your friends to prod you and wake you up. Seek the sacraments diligently, for they are the fountains of life. Don't forget that in this case, God and the world for once agree—neither kingdom can be won without taking it by force.

ELEVEN

# Humility

The saints all agree that true humility is the foundation for every virtue because it is the child of pure love and because it is truth itself.

There are only two real truths — the almightiness of God and the nothingness of his creatures. If your humility is real, you stay in your proper place, content to be nothing. Jesus tells you to be gentle in your heart. Gentleness is the child of humility, just as anger is the child of pride. Only Jesus can give you this, his own true humility of heart. It comes as his gift. It's not a matter of outward works of humility, however exceptional these may be at the proper time, but simply of remaining where God has placed you.

People who imagine themselves to be humble are not truly humble, nor are those who seek anything for themselves. The truly humble so entirely forget themselves that they don't think about themselves. They're *inwardly* humble. They speak of themselves as they would of others. They don't pretend to ignore themselves while they are actually bursting with self-consciousness. They offer themselves for the sake of love, not thinking about how it might appear as humility or pride, not worrying about whether others find their actions lacking in humility.

You must not judge humility by outward appearances, by this action or the other action. It can only be judged by love. Pure love strips away the self and clothes you instead with Jesus so that "it is no longer you that lives, but Christ that lives in you."

In the church, people are always trying to become something great, to be as prominent in the things of religion as they were in the things of the world. Why? Because they crave to be noticed in both contexts. However, the truly humble seek no praise for themselves. Praise and blame are all the same to them. Wherever God puts them, there they remain, never even thinking about looking for something else.

Many people practice outward humility while they are still a long way from this sort of heartfelt humility. However, outward humility that does not flow out from love is false. The more that false humility lowers itself outwardly, the higher it raises itself inwardly. People who admire their own humility are actually proud. Their false humility is a subtle way for them to lift themselves even higher. There will be none of this false humility in heaven. That must give way to simple love.

Those who are filled with Jesus cannot consciously humble themselves because they already feel lower than any possible humiliation. They're not hurt or humiliated by the contempt or blame of others, nor are they lifted up by any praise they receive. They believe that people can never be brought lower than the state where they actually are. Only Jesus was lowered in his incarnation, which is why the scriptures say the he "emptied himself." That cannot be said about earthly creatures.

Many deceive themselves about humility. They try to become humble through their own efforts. Failing to resign themselves to God's will and renounce their interests, they sin against divine love, without which there can be no humility. They are raising themselves up with the same works that they think make them humble. They puff themselves up with the pride of humility and take pride in the humble acts they perform.

The truly humble allow themselves to be carried here or there, content for God to do whatever he chooses for them, like a straw in the wind. There is more true humility in accepting even greatness in this spirit than there is in thwarting God's plans with pretended lowliness. Those who choose to be low rather than lifted up are not necessarily humble, even if they want to be. Those who allow themselves to go up or down—not caring if they're praised or blamed, not listening to what is said about them—are the truly humble, whatever others may think, because they only do what God chooses.

The truly humble ask for nothing and refuse nothing—not from conscious reasons but from such complete self-forgetfulness that they don't consider the matter. The truly humble are those children of whom our Lord says, "the kingdom of heaven belongs to ones like these." An infant doesn't know what it wants. It can't make plans and can do nothing on its own. It can only allow itself to be carried about. This is how you must boldly give yourself to God. If God doesn't use you, that is just. You yourself are good for nothing. If he chooses to use you for some great endeavor, that is for his own glory. Like Mary, you say, "He has done great things for me. He has regarded my lowliness."

False humility believes itself unworthy of God's goodness and doesn't dare to trust it. True humility sees its own unworthiness and gives itself up to God, never doubting that God will work out the best results for it and in it. If God's success depended on you, you might indeed fear that your sins have destroyed any chance you had. However, God needs nothing from you. He will never find anything of value there except for what he himself has placed within you.

Don't be afraid, then, that your past faithlessness makes you unworthy of God's mercy. Nothing is as worthy of his mercy as utter weakness. Jesus came from heaven to earth to seek sinners, not just people. He came to find those who are lost, as indeed everyone is except for him. The doctor seeks the sick, not the healthy. Oh, how God loves those who come boldly to him in their disgusting, ragged clothes and ask — like they would ask a father — for clothes that are worthy of him.

You hesitate to be draw near to God until he shows you a smiling face. I say that if you open your heart completely to him, you will stop worrying about how he looks upon you. Let him show you a harsh, disappointed face if he chooses. He never loves you more than when he is hostile to you, for he is only hostile in order to humble you and set you apart for his service.

Do you want the comfort that God gives, or do you want God himself? If it's the first, then you don't love God for his own sake but for yours. If, however, you seek him alone, you will more truly find him when he judges you than when he comforts you. When he comforts you, you have reason to fear that you might cling more to his sweetness than to him. When he deals roughly with you and you still hold on, you cling to him alone.

How people deceive themselves! They feast in delight when they're aware of God's sweetness, imagining themselves in a seventh heaven, lost in a dream. However, if their faith grows barren and cold, they lose heart, thinking that all is lost when in fact that is the time for real progress if they do not yield to discouragement.

You must leave everything to God. It's not your business to decide how God should deal with you. He knows better than you what's good for you. You deserve a certain amount of trial and barrenness. Bear it patiently. God does his part when he pushes you away. Try to do your part, too, which is to love him without waiting for him to demonstrate his love. Your faithfulness will disarm him and turn all his harshness into tenderness.

However, even if he doesn't become tender, you must still give yourself up to him no matter how he deals with you. You must humbly accept his intention of nailing you to the cross, of bringing you into the desolation of Jesus, his beloved son. This is the food of pure faith and generous love that will sustain your soul. I pray that God will make you strong and lively in the midst of your troubles. Expect everything, and everything will be given to you.

# Twelve

# Learning

Those who choose to be satisfied with themselves because they're guided by reason rather than emotion or desire are wasting their time. They will never arrive at any satisfactory outcome. This is because they can never be sure that emotion or desire isn't secretly moving them while they imagine themselves to be acting from pure reason.

It is God's will to keep you in the dark concerning even the natural order of things on earth. How much more must you then be content to do without evidence and certainty when it comes to the most delicate workings of grace in the deep darkness of faith and the supernatural. This kind of restless, obstinate search for an unattainable certainty is clearly the work of human nature, not grace. You can't guard against it too much. It is a subtle inquiry that will take a hundred shapes. This craving for mathematical certainty takes root in you because of your natural inclinations, your life-long and dedicated study, your habits that are now second nature, and because of your honest desire to guard against delusion. However, religious vigilance should never disturb the peace of your heart or demand evidence to prove the secret workings of grace when it pleases God to keep those things hidden behind a veil.

You know that you should be wary about your tendency to overthink the common matters of everyday life. You should be even more wary about overthinking matters that are higher than reason, matters that God conceals. The more faithful you are in killing your intellectual pursuits, your theological research, your worldly wisdom, your speculations and efforts to convince others, the more you kill your actual, natural frailty and in doing so advance the life of grace within you.

Listen steadfastly to God, and don't willingly listen to yourself on matters that engage your intellect. Only God's grace, working powerfully in a soul, can give you an insight about yourself that is opposed to yourself. He provides this when he finds the soul ready to throw off anything that might hinder it from walking in God's paths. May you never look back! May his will be your will in all things.

It doesn't matter where God's insight and strength come from. God supplies what he chooses from where he chooses. Naaman could not be healed by any of the waters of Syria but was forced to wash in a river of Palestine. The only important things is the source, not the channel. The insight that strengthens your faith, uproots your worldly wisdom, overthrows your self-regard, and humbles you is the best according to God's designs for you. Accept

81

what he sends, and accept it as coming from the Spirit, which "blows where it chooses." It's not for you to know where it comes from or where it goes. You shouldn't try to find what God has hidden but to instead be faithfully attentive to what he reveals.

If you can wean yourself from idle curiosity and superficial reasoning, you gain a great deal of time for meditation and for business. The spirit of prayer makes you simple, concise, clear, self-controlled in thought and word, and calm under pressure. The self is active, verbose, wavering, impulsive, distracted, forever trying to do the impossible. It loses sight of the end because of the means, because of trying to convince, please, and pacify everyone. The spirit of grace calmly tries to do nothing but remain faithful, not fearing that faithfulness will fail to overcome all obstacles. This is the peace that the world can neither give you nor take away, the peace that exceeds all human thought. How could the world give it? The world neither understands it nor believes that it exists in those who enjoy it.

Intellectual argument is a great waste of your energy. The friends of reason, the learned ones who do not pray, extinguish the inner life like the wind blows out a candle. After spending time with them, your heart feels withered, and your mind feels unbalanced. You should avoid these people. They are diseased and contagious.

Some may appear to be inwardly wise, but they are not really so. It's easy to mistake a certain spirit of imagination for inner wisdom. They're focused on the outward matters that they care about deeply, but their zeal hinders them because they continually argue—subtly, exhaustively, and perpetually—about the same points. They have no inner peace, the silence within which God's voice is heard, and thus they're more contagious than others because their errors are more disguised. If you look closely, you find them restless, critical, angry, obsessed with externals, hardened, bitter, proud, full of self, and impatient with contradiction. They are a sort of spiritual gadfly—disturbed by everything and almost always disturbing others.

The people you used to listen to were infinitely barren, rationalistic, critical, and opposed to the interior life. If you listen to them even a little now, you will soon become entangled in their endless arguments. A dangerous attraction will drag you back from grace into the depths of your natural weakness. Former habits are easily renewed, and falling back into your old failings is so easy that you notice it less than most other changes. Guard against this. Look out for the first steps backward that can lead to all the rest.

Those who study should treat it as a true calling of God. They should work at it like people who go to the store for what they need, day after day. All their study should be done in a spirit of prayer. God is at once truth and love. You can't really know the truth unless you love it. Those who love truth well understand it well. Those who don't love Love itself don't understand it, either. Those who love much and live humbly in their ignorance are loved by truth. They understand things that the worldly wise don't even want to know. This is the sort of learning that I desire for you, a field of study that is revealed to little children and infants and hidden from the learned and wise.

What I wish for you is better than anything you can fear to lose. Be faithful in what you know, and in this way, you are deserving of further knowledge. Mistrust your intellect, which has so often deceived you. Be simple, and be firm in your simplicity. "The world in its present form is passing away," and you pass away with it if you conform to its vanities. The truth of God endures forever, and you are stable if you steadfastly remain in his truth.

Blessed are those who are truly set free! No one but the Son of God can set you free. He does so by breaking every chain that holds you back, by using the sword to divide husband and wife, father and son, brother and sister. The world then means nothing to you. However, as long as the world holds you, "freedom" is just a word. You are like a bird whose feet are held by a string. The bird appears to be free, but because it can't fly beyond the length of its cord, it is a prisoner.

# THIRTEEN

# Simplicity

There is a simplicity that is merely a weakness, and there is a simplicity that is a wonderful virtue. Sometimes simplicity comes from a lack of perception and ignorance about what's appropriate. In the world, when people call anyone "simple," they generally mean a foolish, ignorant person. However, true simplicity, far from being foolish, is almost sublime. All good people like and admire it, see it in others, and know what it involves, yet they can't precisely define it. You might say about simplicity what *The Imitation of Christ* says about contrition: "I would rather experience it than know how to define it."

I say that simplicity is an honesty of soul that prevents self-consciousness.

Simplicity is not the same as sincerity, which is a less advanced virtue. Many people say nothing but what they believe is true and don't try to appear to be anything but what they are. However, they're also afraid of appearing to be something they're *not*, so they're constantly thinking about themselves, judging every word and thought, worrying about having done too much or too little. These people are sincere, but they're not simple. They're not comfortable around others, nor are others comfortable around them. God's judgment is the same. He doesn't like souls that are so self-absorbed, who are always looking at themselves in the mirror.

This kind of false wisdom, in spite of its seriousness, is almost as vain and foolish as the foolishness of those who plunge headlong into worldly pleasure. One is intoxicated by outward surroundings, and the other by inward self-consciousness, but both are still drunk. The second condition is worse, though, because these people don't try to be cured. On the contrary, they pride themselves on it and feel that it makes them better than others.

Real simplicity lies in a happy medium that is equally free from both thoughtlessness and pretension. You're not so overwhelmed by outward things that you're unable to reflect inwardly, but neither are you lost in the endless little inward refinements of self-consciousness. You see where you're going but don't lose any time thinking about every little step or looking back at what you've done. That is true simplicity.

The first step toward simplicity is for you to set aside outward things and look within to understand your own true interests. This much is entirely correct and natural, a wise self-love that desires to avoid the intoxication of the world.

The next step is to add the consideration of God to your consideration of self. This is only a small step toward true wisdom because you're still so self-focused. You won't be satisfied by this.

You want to be sure that you fear God and worry that you don't. That sends you into an endless cycle of self-examination. This restless focus on the self is far from the peace and freedom of real love. When God begins to open your heart to receive something higher and purer, it's time then to follow the works of his power, step by step, and thus enter into true simplicity.

The third step is to leave behind your restless self-examination and focus on God instead. Gradually, your soul begins to forget itself. You become filled with God and stop feeding on yourself. In this condition, you're no longer blind to your own failings or unconcerned with your sins. Indeed, you're more conscious of them than ever before. Greater light exposes your sins in plainer form. However, this self-knowledge comes from God rather than yourself, so it is neither restless nor uncomfortable.

When all your self-examination and brooding is thus overcome, your soul acquires indescribable peace and freedom. I can write about this, but only by experiencing it do you learn what it really is. When you reach this stage, you're like a child at its mother's breast, free from fear or longing, comfortable to be moved here or there, unconcerned about what others may think—except for the way that love doesn't want to create obstacles for others. In this state, you do everything as well as possible, cheerfully and confidently and entirely unconcerned with success or failure. As Paul says, "I don't care how I'm judged by you or by any human standard. I don't even judge myself."

"But how," you ask, "can I help being constantly self-absorbed when a crowd of anxious thoughts troubles me and makes me self-conscious?" I only ask you to do what you can already do. Don't voluntarily yield to these thoughts. Once you become aware of them, resist them. If you resist them steadily, you gradually become free them. Trying to repress thoughts of self is in practice a continual self-consciousness, and that only distracts you from your duties and holds you back from experiencing the presence of God.

*Freedom from the World*

The main thing is to submit all your interests, pleasures, comfort, and renown to God. Those who unreservedly accept whatever God chooses to give them in this world—humiliations, problems, trials from within, and trials from without—make great progress towards victory over self. They don't fear praise or disapproval. If they find themselves wincing at something, they treat it so off-handedly that their sensitivity soon dies away. This kind of complete submission is true freedom, and from it comes true simplicity.

You ask, "Am I never to think about myself or about what affects me?" Indeed, no. I don't ask you to be that restrained. In fact, that attempt at simplicity destroys true simplicity. What should you do then? Make no rules for yourself at all. Try instead to avoid pretending to be something you are not. When you're inclined to talk about yourself out of self-consciousness, resist that itching desire by quietly turning your attention to God or to some duty that he gives you. When you feel inclined to talk about yourself out of vanity, the only thing to do is stop as soon as you can. If there *is* some real reason for talking about yourself, then get right to the point.

When it's necessary to talk about yourself, learn to speak as honestly and simply about yourself as others, just as Paul often talks about himself in his letters. He refers to his birth and his Roman citizenship. He says that he was "not in the least inferior to the most eminent apostles," that he has done even more than them, that he withstood Peter to his face because Peter was in the wrong. Paul says that he had been "brought up into paradise and heard inexpressible things, things that no one is permitted to tell." He says that he "always take pains to have a clear conscience toward both God and man," and that he "worked harder than any of the other apostles." He teaches the faithful to be "followers of me, just as I am of Jesus."

See how he talks about himself with such dignity and simplicity. He can say even the loftiest things without displaying any emotion or self-consciousness. He talks about himself as he would talk about things that had happened a thousand years earlier.

True simplicity like this affects all things, including your outward manner, and makes you natural and unpretentious. You get used to acting in a straightforward way, which is incomprehensible to those who are always self-occupied and artificial. This outward manner may sometimes appear to be a little too comfortable and care-free, but because it's characterized by a truthful, gentle, innocent, cheerful, and calm simplicity, it's quite attractive.

Worldly wisdom despises this kind of simplicity, and oh, how this kind of simplicity despises the world! As Paul says, "Those who live according to the flesh have their minds set on what the flesh desires. Those who live in the Spirit have their minds set on what the Spirit desires." True simplicity is "the pearl of great price" in the holy scriptures. I would give everything I own to have it.

FOURTEEN

# Holiness

Holiness is not the harsh, wearisome restraint that you imagine. It requires you to belong to God with your whole heart, and once that is the case, whatever you do for him becomes easy. You're always happy as long as you keep an undivided will, desiring only what he desires, willing to do whatever he requires. You gladly give up everything else, and you reap a hundred-fold harvest — peace of conscience, freedom of mind, the sweetness of giving yourself entirely to God, the joy of seeing his light grow brighter within your heart, and freedom from the world's slavery. This is the blessedness that God's true children possess, even in the midst of suffering, when they remain faithful.

True, you must sacrifice yourself, but you sacrifice yourself to the one you love best. You must suffer, but you suffer willingly, and you would rather bear this suffering than the unreal pleasures of the world. Your body may be racked with pain, your mind harassed, you spirit weak and anxious, but your will is firm and steady within you. You can utter a steadfast "amen!" to every blow that comes from the hand of God. When you have such a mind as this, everything becomes good. The most trivial pursuits are turned into good works.

How happy you are when you give yourself to God! You're set free from slavery to your own desires. You're set free from the judgment of the worldly, from the meanness and tyranny of their rules, and from their chilling, heartless mockery. You're set free from the sorrows that the world attributes to fate, from the fickleness of friends, from the traps of enemies, and from your own weakness. You're freed from the uncertainty of life, from the terror of an ungodly death, from the bitter remorse of sinful pleasure, and finally, from God's eternal condemnation.

True Christians, come what may, accept whatever happens to them and want nothing to hold them back. You must therefore learn to scorn earthly things for God's purposes. I don't say that you abandon them entirely. The difference is that now you do these things to serve and please God instead of serving and pleasing the world and yourself.

Jesus says to all Christians, "Leave behind your foolish ways, take up your cross, and follow me." You must not remain attached to the world, which God condemns because if its sins. These truths are difficult for many people because they only see what religion requires, not what it offers. They ignore the loving Spirit who makes everything easy. They don't understand that the way to the highest holiness is a path so loving and peaceful that all efforts are easy.

All excuses for holding back from God are rejected by the commandment to "love the Lord your God with all your heart, and with all your soul, and with all your strength, and with all your mind." God allows no division between you and him. There is only one way of loving God, and that way does not try to bargain with God. It accepts every inspiration of God's with an open and generous heart. If you claim to have this love but hold onto the world with one hand, you run the risk of finding yourself among those lukewarm Christians whom God says he will "spit out of his mouth." He can't stand cowardly souls who say to themselves, "I will go this far, but no further."

You can't stop at learning the general will of God, either. You must seek to understand his will in detail, to know what pleases him the most and what is the most holy way. You're only acting as a rational creature when you consider God's general will and then adapt it to fit your will. There is no other true light to follow. Anything else is just a fantasy, a bit of burning straw.

Worldly people understand that they're not happy, and they hope to become happy through the very things that make them miserable. They're unhappy because of what they lack, and what they have can't satisfy them. Their troubles are real, but their joys are fleeting, hollow, and bitter. To them, life is one long experience of sin, with eternal judgment hanging over their heads. Their unreal happiness will quickly become unending tears and groans. Life is like a passing shadow for them—or at best, like a flower that springs up in the morning, dries up in the day, and is trampled before nightfall.

The terrible thing is that so many thousands blind themselves, shunning the light that condemns their works of darkness. They chose the life that belongs to creatures, the life that dies with the body, and they refuse to live any other life. They degrade themselves more and more in order to stifle their shame and remorse. They ridicule people who think seriously. They say that those who strive to live in God are fools.

What can be done to rouse them from this pitiable condition? They must pray for light.

They must realize the depth of God's mercy and the depth of their own fallen nature. Then they will finally hate themselves, renounce themselves, throw themselves upon God, and be lost in him. Blessed loss, in which they find their true selves! There is no more self-seeking, but everything works to their benefit because "all things work together for good for those who love God," and who are filled with his Spirit.

No Christian really lacks the Spirit except for those who don't ask for it or who don't ask correctly. It is not with words or with outward actions that you secure the Spirit of life, without whom even the best works are lifeless. The Spirit comes through the heart's desire, through a thorough rejection of self before God. God is so good. He waits only for your heart to desire him and then fills you to overflowing with the gift that is himself. He says that the prayer is not even on the lips — scarcely formed by the heart — before he grants the request. However, it is the heart's prayer that he answers.

In God's presence, you understand the emptiness of this world, which will soon pass away like
a cloud. All worldly grandeur and displays of
power will vanish like a dream. The proud will be
humbled, the powerful will become helpless, and
the mighty will kneel before the eternal majesty of
God. On his day of judgment, God will outshine
everything that glitters in the world, replacing
these flickering lights like the sun replaces star-
light. You will see nothing but God then. Try as
you might, you will find nothing but him.

Is it worth your time to cling to such a world
as this? It's a world that you have to leave almost
as soon as you enter, a phantom, a "shadow that
disappears." You frail and foolish world, shame
on you for dazzling people with your showy
cheapness! Your smile can't hide the pain you
bring them. You disappear in a moment, yet you
dare to promise joy. There is no joy for anyone
except for those who see your emptiness in the
light of Jesus.

* 9 7 8 1 6 3 1 7 1 0 0 5 6 *